HOT RODS AND DRAGSTERS

BY MELVYN RECORD

CHARTWELL
BOOKS, INC.

A QUINTET BOOK

ISBN: 0-7858-0342-4

This book was designed and produced by
Quintet Publishing Limited
6, Blundell Street
London N7 9BH

Creative Director: Richard Dewing
Designer: Stuart Walden
Project Editor: Damien Thompson
Editor: John Clark
Editorial Adviser: Lorraine Gunter
Picture Researchers: Leslie Lovett and Melvyn Record
Jacket Design: Nik Morley

Typeset in Great Britain by
Central Southern Typesetters, Eastbourne
Manufactured in China by
Regent Publishing Services Limited.

This edition produced for sale in the USA,
its territories and dependencies only.

Published by Chartwell Books
A Division of Book Sales, Inc.
P.O. Box 7100
Edison, New Jersey 08818–7100

CONTENTS

REVVING THE CHANGES

If ever a sport was destined to be full of record breakers, drag racing is that sport. Constant technological and mechanical progress has enabled these hot rods – which compete in a variety of categories, from Top Fuel to Super Street – to cover the standing-start quarter-mile in less than five seconds in 1991. In 1951, the standard run was just over 11 seconds.

Created by American hot rodders of the late 1940s and early 1950s, drag racing has progressed from an outlawed pastime to a fully-fledged motorsport boasting more than half a million competitors worldwide racing for millions of dollars in prize money.

By the mid-1960s, all but a few of the categories that are raced in today were created. During the late 1960s and most of the 1970s, the sport shed its racing-circus image and entered the 1980s as one of the more professional of all sports.

Despite competition from rival sanctioning organizations, the Los Angeles, California-based National Hot Rod Association (NHRA) and its Winston Championship Drag Racing series are the standards for all other hot-rodding and drag-racing clubs. Created by Wally Parks in 1951, the NHRA celebrated its 30th anniversary as the largest motor-sports association in the world. More than 80,000 members and a weekly drag-racing programme that allows more than 450,000 racers to compete in North America alone helps the NHRA maintain its world-leading stature.

If a first-time spectator at a drag race remembers just one image, it will be the Top Fuel dragster, the ultimate hot rod. With big wheels at the rear and small wheels at the front, the 4,000-horsepower, 295-mph (475-km/h) hot rods are indeed unchained lightning on the racetrack.

▶ **Smoke billowing from his dragster's rear tyres, Canadian Craig Smith performs all hot-rod fans' favourite pre-race ceremony: the burnout.**

▲ **The Christmas tree, perhaps the single most symbolic image to all hot rodders. When the green light blinks, all self-respecting hot rodders mash the gas pedal.**

◀ **When hot rodders took their act to the dry lakes and disused airfields, their cars quickly became stripped down chassis, eventually evolving into what became known as dragsters.**

Drag racing is as American as apple pie. Originally considered a temporary fad, it is one of few sports to originate in the new West to stand the test of time and be transferred to other continents.

As the sport advances towards the 21st century, racers the world over are still trying to beat the driver in the other lane to the finishing line. Far from being an exclusively American sport, racers from Australia, Britain, Finland, Norway and Sweden – to name but a few countries – have been travelling the straight-line quarter-mile since the early 1960s.

The American origins and continued American influence on the sport cannot be underestimated. Racers in Europe and Australasia aspire to be as competitive as their American counterparts. All the hardware used on their respective hot rods – from clutches to rear-wing struts and engines – originates in America. American influence is also evident in the language of the sport.

THE FIRST RACES
★ ★ ★

Reports are many and conflicting as to exactly when and where the first drag race took place. Australian Top Fuel racer Jim Read says that he read an article about "hot rods racing over a straight-line quarter-mile on Blackpool [England] pleasure beach" in a newspaper dated August 1936. No matter where the sport originated, its spiritual home is in southern California.

By the time C.J. "Pappy" Hart opened the first commercial dragstrip at Orange County Airport in Santa Ana, California, in 1951, the hot rodders already had been fine-tuning their racing techniques for 15 years or more.

▲ **With their visually exciting colours and shapes – and their near unbelievable on-track performance –** **dragsters attract armchair hot rodders in their thousands across the world.**

The first drag races were clandestine affairs, usually conducted on quiet back roads outside main towns or from one set of traffic lights to the next through town along the main drag (hence the term drag racing). Racing on the public street, however, was not popular with the local police. With their encouragement, the hot rodders were ushered to local dry lakes or to many of the abandoned airfields left in southern California after World War II.

That move proved to be a blessing in disguise for the hot rodders because they were now able to express themselves more freely. Away from the confines of public roads and no longer concerned with keeping their hot rods "streetable", the cars quickly became stripped-down chassis bearing little or no resemblance to their former selves. The quest for quicker elapsed times and faster speeds became as important as beating the car in the other lane.

By the late 1940s, the sport of hot rodding – or drag racing, as it was becoming more widely known – was gaining in popularity, not just in southern California but all over the country, thanks in no small way to a new magazine created to report on this latest craze called *Hot Rod*.

WALLY PARKS – A FOUNDING FATHER

It could be argued that without Wally Parks' influence, drag racing never may have become a legitimate sport. It certainly would not have advanced to its current level of being a major motorsports activity enjoyed by hundreds of thousands of racers and fans. Parks was a test driver for General Motors before World War II, already establishing himself as a chap who liked fast cars by racing competitively at California's Muroc dry lake in the 1930s and 1940s.

Realizing that the fledgling sport of hot rodding, or drag racing, needed organizing, Parks with Ak Miller and Marvin Lee, created the National Hot Rod Association (NHRA) in 1951. They could not have known it at the time, but the NHRA would become the largest motorsports sanctioning body in the world and would continue to set the standard for straight-line performance competition as motor racing moves into the 21st century.

GOING LEGIT
★ ★ ★

One of the founding editors of *Hot Rod* magazine, Wally Parks, also had the intention of creating the National Hot Rod Association (NHRA), a club whose main task would be to bring some organization and order to the sport of drag racing.

By May 1951, the NHRA was a reality, complete with rules, membership fees, and an emblem that would become synonymous with championship drag racing. Parks' main objective was to establish the sport as a bona fide motor-racing pastime that could be conducted in as safe a fashion as possible.

From these humble beginnings was spawned the NHRA Safety Safari (originally Drag Safari), a group of NHRA founders who toured North America's dragstrips, which were springing up almost weekly, to make sure that at least the safety standards were being adhered to. In most

▲ **The NHRA Safety Safari was founded in the early 1950s to create a safe place for the hot rodders to race. Five decades later it has evolved into an organization that specializes in everything from track preparation to rescuing drivers from errant race cars.**

◄ **From a plan to get the hot rodders off the streets and into a safer environment, Wally Parks has watched the National Hot Rod Association (NHRA) grow into the largest motor racing sanctioning organization in the world.**

► By the mid-1970s, drag racing had long since outgrown the dry lakes and abandoned runways for purpose-built race tracks, such as Orange County International Raceway (OCIR) in California. Unfortunately for OCIR, it fell victim to ever-expanding urban development – like many other southern California racing facilities.

▼ The ultimate hot rod. Thanks to 40 years refinement, the early dragsters of the late 1940s and early 1950s have turned into 300-inch (762-cm) wheelbase, 4,000 horsepower vehicles that are the most powerful landlocked race cars on earth.

cases, the conduct of the meetings was little more than a formality, although the standards of the vehicles did leave a bit to be desired.

The quickest cars of the day were capable of covering the quarter-mile from a standing start in about 10.5 seconds with finishing-line speeds approaching 140 mph (225.30 km/h). The experts of the time calculated that the quickest a vehicle would ever cover the track would be in around nine seconds flat, with maximum speeds of around 170 mph (273.58 km/h).

During the next 35 years, drag racing grew from a sport contested by leather-jacketed hot rodders to an exhibition watched by more than a million spectators a year. Drag racing rivals Formula 1 and Championship Auto Racing Teams (CART) racing in terms of spectator appeal, and although it still cannot boast the corporate interest of those two types of competition, NHRA Championship Drag Racing manages to net more than $18-million per year series. Parks' dream of legitimizing the sport has long since been realized.

▶ Tom Hoover, destined to become one of drag racing's truly international stars in the early 1980s, started his career behind the wheel of a front-engined dragster in the late 1960s. The car was capable of mid-six-second performances with speeds approaching 230 mph (370 km/h).

"BIG DADDY"

★ ★ ★

If one man's name is synonymous with drag racing, it is that of Don "Big Daddy" Garlits. A drag racer since the mid-1950s, Garlits' influence on the sport is still felt today even though he no longer races. Winner of 35 NHRA National event titles during a career spanning nearly 30 years, Garlits has spread the word of drag racing across the globe and inspired racers in Europe and Australia.

Garlits is credited with making the rear-engined dragster as popular as it is today after he changed to one following a clutch explosion in his slingshot dragster at Lions Dragstrip in California in 1971. Although the rear-engine concept had been tried several times before, Garlits was the first racer to make the configuration successful.

By the 1980s, Top Fuel dragsters had stagnated and the class was slowly but surely dying a death of chronic lack of interest. Don Garlits

▲ **Primitive by 1990s standards, Don Garlits' Wynn's Charger dragster was the standard bearer when the sport entered the 1980s. With this car Garlits set one of the longest-standing performance records in drag-racing history, a 5.63-second lap at the 1975 Winston Finals. The run was the fastest ever recorded for more than six years.**

▶ **Compared to Don Garlits' 1975 record-breaking dragster, Junior Kaiser's Top Fuel entry looks as though it comes from another century. About the only thing the two cars have in common is that they are of similar configuration.**

◀ **No one person had his name on more race cars than Keith Black; his aluminium Chrysler V-8-based engined powered more dragsters than any other manufacturer's. A former boat racer, Black turned his attentions to the ever-expanding hot rod market in the early 1950s and remained the sport's leading engine supplier through four decades. Black died on May 13, 1991.**

had established a National elapsed time record for the class at 5.637 seconds four-and-a-half years earlier on 11 October 1975 at the Ontario Motor Speedway, California, and drivers had yet to better it.

"The reason that my 5.63 held up for so long was that I was doing some things (mechanically) that were not normal," Garlits explained. Garlits was running a lot of compression, a larger volume of fuel, more overdrive on the supercharger, and more ignition. He also had a higher

◄ Apart from Keith Black, the sport's other engine builder of note was the late Joe Pisano. Creator of the JP-1 aluminium Chrysler-based engine, Pisano also specialized in piston manufacture. Pisano died in late July, 1991.

gear ratio and was running a special set of tyres that he had recently obtained in Indianapolis.

"Unfortunately, I wasn't able to continue with that combination because it was extremely hard on parts. I ruined two motors at that (Ontario) event. We didn't have the connecting rods or fuel pumps to withstand what I was trying to do, and I was running a set of stock Dodge aluminum heads."

Another factor hurting Garlits was the lack of a major sponsor, so he had to stop his expensive experiments with parts before the car bled him completely dry.

After his victory at the 1975 World Finals, Garlits all but disappeared off the face of the earth. Dissatisfied with the way NHRA was running the sport, he retired (as he did many times), then returned and ran primarily in the AHRA ranks, although he did make occasional appearances at NHRA National events in the early 1980s.

NHRA 250-MPH CLUB

For reasons that seemed like a good idea at the time, the NHRA created the 250-mph Club, which would honour the first eight drivers to exceed that magic speed (equal to 402.33 km/h). It took a long time for the Club to be filled — longer perhaps than even the NHRA anticipated. Don Garlits recorded the historic first speed of more than 250 mph, 250.69 (403.44 km/h) at the 1975 World Finals, and it took until Mark Oswald ran 256.41 (412.64 km/h) in the Candies & Hughes dragster at the 1982 NorthStar Nationals for the Club to be filled.

Perhaps the most impressive member of the Club is Billy Meyer, whose 254.95-mph (410.29-km/h) clocking at the 1982 Summernationals was recorded in his Funny Car, the only car of its class to make the Club.

Also of interest, Jerry Ruth's 255.68-mph (411.47-km/h) lap was recorded in one of Garlits' dragsters while "Big Daddy" was racing at a match race in England.

		mph	km/h	
1	DON GARLITS	250.69	403.44	11 Oct. 1975
2	JERRY RUTH	255.68	411.47	9 July 1977
3	RICHARD THARP	250.69	403.44	3 Sept. 1977
4	S. MULDOWNEY	255.58	411.30	3 Feb. 1978
5	GARY BECK	250.00	402.33	7 Oct. 1978
6	DAVE UYEHARA	250.00	402.33	7 Oct. 1978
7	BILLY MEYER	254.95	410.29	17 July 1982
8	MARK OSWALD	256.41	412.64	20 Aug. 1982

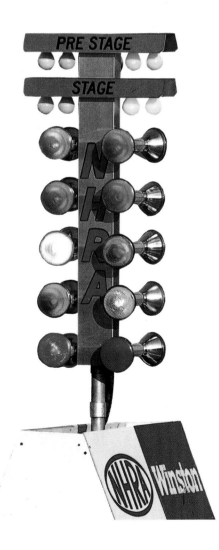

MAN AHEAD OF HIS TIME

★ ★ ★

By the dawn of the new decade, Garlits was experimenting with a big-nosed entry, dubbed Godzilla by the motorsports press. But he was still no closer to bettering his own 5.63-second record. The closest he came was at the 1982 Gatornationals, one of those occasional visits to the NHRA tour, when he recorded 5.72 seconds.

Shirley Muldowney had replaced Garlits as the sport's resident superstar. The charismatic racer from Michigan had already won the 1977 Winston Top Fuel title, and won it again in 1980.

As testimony to today's advanced technology, Muldowney's Championship-winning car would have trouble qualifying for an Alcohol Dragster field in the 1990s. Her 1980 Valvoline-backed dragster boasted a 250-inch (635-cm) wheelbase chassis from Ron Attebury's workshop. It had a stubby rear wing, a two-speed transmission, and a

JEB ALLEN – *1981 WINSTON TOP FUEL CHAMPION*

When Jeb Allen won the 1972 Summernationals, he was just 17 years old and on his way to a successful career as a Top Fuel

dragster racer. Nine years later, when he drove his Praying Mantis dragster to the Winston Top Fuel title, Allen had become recognized as a force to be reckoned with.

Allen was hot right from the beginning, winning the season-opening Winternationals by beating Marvin Graham in the final. At the Gatornationals, Allen hit 5.62 seconds, 250.69 mph (403.44 km/h) during qualifying to become the first driver to eclipse Don Garlits' six-year record run of 5.63. Further notable victories followed at the Cajun Nationals, Mile-High Nationals and Golden Gate Nationals.

Allen's bank account began to dry up towards the end of the season, and he was forced to take a conservative approach to his racing operation. That enabled Shirley Muldowney and, towards the end of the season, Gary Beck, to close the gap at the head of the points table.

However, when Muldowney lost in the first round of eliminations at the season-ending Winston Finals and Beck failed to set Top Speed of the Meet in the final round against Dwight Salisbury, Allen was crowned Champion by just 31 points – an exciting finale to a three-horse contest.

CHASSIS: Ron Attebury
ENGINE: 8 cylinder aluminium Keith Black
CAPACITY: 484 cu in (7.9 L)
COMPUTER-CALCULATED HORSEPOWER: 3,000 bhp @ 6,800 rpm
CYLINDER HEADS: 2-valve Stage II
FUEL CONSUMED PER RUN: 1.06 gallons per second
TYRES: Goodyear
SPONSORS: English Leather
BEST TIME: 5.62 seconds
BEST SPEED: 254.23 mph
EVENT VICTORIES: Winternationals 5.92 seconds 229.59 mph; Mile-High Nationals 5.94 seconds 243.24 mph; Golden Gate Nationals 14.46 seconds 49.80 mph

◄ **Many attempts have been made at refining, and even improving on the current drag racing power plant that evolved from an aluminium Chrysler V-8. The Australian McGee Brothers' engine is a quad-cam unit that burns an enormous amount of fuel, but is also somewhat heavy on parts. The experimental engine ran a 5.08-second best at the 1989 Winternationals.**

◄ **(Inset) The aluminium V-8 engine requires a substantial amount of attention, particularly between rounds of racing, when everything is inspected on the engine to check for any burns or scuffs. This kind of maintenance has been one of the reasons for the increased performance and consistency of the top-fuel dragsters.**

flimsy clutch. The nitromethane fuel was fed into the engine by a single fuel pump, and the air/fuel mixture was ignited by a single magneto. On a good run, Muldowney would stop the clocks at somewhere around 5.80 seconds with finishing-line speeds of approximately 250 mph (402.33 km/h).

The car that carried Joe Amato to the 1990 Winston title is as far removed from Muldowney's Championship-winning entry as a Ferrari

is from a Mini Metro. Basically, the only things the two have in common are four wheels, a steering wheel and a driver's seat.

Amato's Valvoline-backed dragster has a 300-inch (762-cm) wheelbase (the maximum allowed by NHRA rules), a swept-back rear wing that has been designed for aerodynamic efficiency, a direct-drive transmission, and a multi-stage clutch that feeds in groups of fingers in stages to maximize its effectiveness. The nitromethane is forced into the engine by two fuel pumps, each of which is capable of pumping more than 25 gallons (94.63 litres) per minute. The air/fuel mixture is ignited by two magnetos (with two spark plugs per cylinder). This set-up is capable of taking Amato from one end of the track to the other in less than five seconds at almost 300 mph (482.79 km/h).

Garlits was essentially five years ahead of his time, and because no racer seemed capable of approaching Garlits' performance, fans and racers lost interest in the class.

However, all hope was not lost on the Kings of the Sport, as the Top Fuel dragsters have become known. Chassis builder Al Swindahl,

◀ **Nicknamed Big Red – for obvious reasons – the Sid Waterman fuel pump helped racers to pump larger amounts of fuel into their engines, thus increasing potential horsepower.**

▼ **It did not take racers too long to reason that if one large-volume fuel pump was good, then two must be better. By 1985 Big Red had outlived its usefulness and racers were already**

experimenting with twin pumps, a set-up that is still adequate as the sport enters the 1990s.

▶ **Another area that undoubtedly helped with the continual push on the performance envelope was improvements in tyre technology. Goodyear enjoys a virtual monopoly in the Top Fuel and Funny Car ranks with its Eagle Dragway Special.**

whose cars would eventually dominate in the 1980s, saw the first of his cars win an NHRA National event when Jerry Ruth won the 1980 Mile-High Nationals in one of the unusual cars; they were unusual because of the driver's seating position which was more upright than lying down. After Canadian Terry Capp won the 1980 U.S. Nationals in another Swindahl-built car, orders began rolling in to the Tacoma, Washington, chassis maker, led by Top Fuel's best-financed operation, the Candies & Hughes team and its driver, Richard Tharp.

Garlits' 5.63 stood the test of time until March 1981, when Jeb Allen, on his way to the Winston Top Fuel title, hit a 5.62 at the Gatornationals. By the year's end, racers had recorded 10 sub-5.70-second runs, all of which were capped by Canadian Gary Beck, who recorded a 5.573 at the season-ending Winston Finals in October.

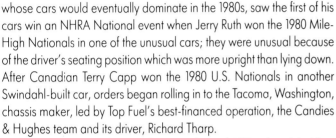

PUMP UP THE VOLUME

★ ★ ★

It did not take the nitro racers long to learn that in drag racing if some is good and more is better, then too much must be just enough. That was especially true when it came to fuel volume. The more fuel that could be crammed into a cylinder and burn, the greater the power output.

Sid Waterman, a racer turned fuel-pump manufacturer, had cornered this particular area of the market. His Big Red pump was the key to Gary Beck's 5.39-second lap in 1983, and Billy Meyer's success in a Funny Car. Beck and Meyer were his two original high-volume fuel-pump customers.

Soon the racers figured that if one pump was good, then two, logically, must be better. By 1985, Big Red had outlived its usefulness and racers such as Kenny Bernstein, Tom McEwen, and Connie Kalitta were experimenting with two pumps, although they were using the lower volume Enderle units. It was not until that year's U.S. Nationals, however, that the true potential of dual pumps was realized. Former Funny Car Champion Raymond Beadle utilized the Enderle dual-metering system on his Blue Max entry that helped driver John Lombardo push aside the opposition. Bernstein won the Budweiser Big Bud Shootout competition, and McEwen was the low qualifier in Funny Car with a 5.67, an elapsed time that three years earlier had been difficult for even a Top Fuel dragster to achieve.

Top fuel racers, understandably, jumped onto the twin-pump band-wagon, and the new system was credited with helping Beck end a 15-month winless stretch at the 1985 Winston Finals.

Tim Richards, crew chief on the Joe Amato entry and destined to become the fuel tuner of the early 1990s, tried the twin pumps along with feeding the fuel lines directly into the cylinder heads.

But tuning the fuel-delivery system was still very much a hit-and-miss affair – as it remains today – and racers like Don Garlits, Gene Snow and Dick LaHaie stuck with the single pump and were still competitive. However, by the turn of the decade, dual pumps and in-head cylinder injection were mandatory for a racer to compete with the cream of the competition. A complex series of check valves and return lines have replaced the once simple set-ups.

LIGHT MY FIRE

★ ★ ★

Pumping extra fuel into the engine is one thing, but burning it all is another. Extra fuel is no use unless it can all be burned, so racers began turning up the wick in the ignition department.

By 1983 the father-and-son team of Connie and Scott Kalitta was already experimenting with 16-plug heads (two spark plugs for each cylinder). When dual fuel-pump fever hit in 1985, so did the nearly obligatory use of dual magnetos to ignite the fuel.

In 1986, Bernstein and his crew chief, former Funny Car racer Dale Armstrong, introduced a set of heads that could accommodate three spark plugs per cylinder. Another Funny Car racer, Billy Meyer, even tried a four-plug head.

Realizing that things were going to get out of hand without a set standard, the NHRA introduced a two-plugs-per-cylinder rule. By 1987, even hard-core single magneto users such as Garlits were using the dual-magneto set-up.

▶ If two magnetos are better, then three must be just enough — or so racers thought. This triple-magneto set (with three spark plugs per cylinder) appeared on Kenny Bernstein's Funny Car early 1986. The unit was quickly legislated out by the NHRA, who feared the racers would get carried away and not stop until they had one magneto per cylinder.

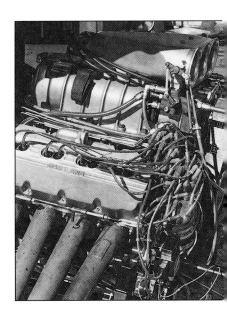

▼ With the introduction of twin fuel pumps, racers found they could not burn the extra fuel fast enough. That particular problem accelerated the introduction of the twin magneto.

GARY BECK – 1983 WINSTON TOP FUEL CHAMPION

There is little argument that 1983 was the year of Gary Beck. Driving Larry Minor's number one car, Beck overcame the opposition like no one had done before and no one has done since. On the way to taking the 1983 Championship title, Beck won four National events: The Gatornationals, Southern Nationals, U.S. Nationals and Golden Gate Nationals. He also set Low Elapsed Time at 10 of the 12 National events held during the season, and he recorded the 17 quickest times in Top Fuel history to that point.

Amazingly, as dominant as Beck was in 1983, he was never to be a factor in the Championship race throughout the rest of his career, and left the Minor team before the 1986 season was over.

CHASSIS: Al Swindahl
ENGINE: 8 cylinder aluminium Keith Black
CAPACITY: 484 cu in (7.9 L)
COMPUTER-CALCULATED HORSEPOWER: 3,500 bhp @ 6,800 rpm
CYLINDER HEADS: 2-valve Dart
FUEL CONSUMED PER RUN: 1.11 gallons per second
TYRES: Goodyear
SPONSORS: Larry Minor Racing
BEST TIME: 5.391 seconds
BEST SPEED: 252.10 mph
EVENT VICTORIES:
Gatornationals 5.49 seconds 251.39 mph; Southern Nationals 5.53 seconds 249.30 mph; Golden Gate Nationals 5.39 seconds 252.10 mph; U.S. Nationals 5.50 seconds 248.61 mph

I'LL HUFF AND I'LL PUFF

★ ★ ★

In the mid-1980s, Norm Drazy, a mechanical engineer, adapted an industrial screw compressor to run as a drag-racing supercharger. The PSI, as it was called (named after Drazy's company, Performance Systems Inc.), was instantly more efficient than previous types. Employing male and female rotors, the PSI compressed air internally before discharging into the manifold.

After the PSI made its debut on Mark Niver's Alcohol Dragster in July 1988, Gary Southern surprised everyone at that year's U.S. Nationals by running a 6.12-second best in his Alcohol Dragster with the PSI. After that race, every big-name alcohol racer ordered a PSI unit.

But the PSI's success was short-lived. Niver's car exploded a unit in July 1989, sending parts hundreds of feet into the air. Despite the mandated use of blower-restraint straps and ballistic bags, another PSI exploded on Mike Troxel's Alcohol Dragster in October 1989, and the PSI was history.

▲ **Perhaps the ultimate in supercharger development was Norm Drazy's PSI screw-type unit. Far more efficient than the conventional Roots-type blower, the PSI dramatically improved the** performance of all cars it ran on. Its success was short-lived, however, as a succession of unexplained explosions led to the PSI being banned.

COMMANDER DATA

★ ★ ★

In the early days of hot rodding and drag racing, the crew chief relied on the driver to tell him what had happened on a particular run. He would then make the necessary tuning changes based on that information. But as elapsed times plummeted and speeds soared, things were happening too quickly for the driver to remember everything.

Data recorders provided the relief the teams were looking for. Several hit the sport in the early 1980s, designed to take the guesswork out of tuning a high-horsepower race car.

Don Prudhomme introduced a CEHCO recorder on his Funny Car at the 1982 Grand Premier event at Orange County International Raceway in Los Angeles, California. A primitive unit, it logged exhaust temperatures and took fuel-pressure readings, basically recording if and when the engine dropped a cylinder or was running too rich or too lean.

Top Fuel racer Ron Smith had the next improvement in data recorders. His self-designed unit measured engine and driveshaft rpm (which provided clutch-slippage data), fuel- and supercharger-pressure readings, and throttle-pedal pressure. The car was also fitted with a fifth wheel to measure ground speed and rear-tyre growth.

Yet it was another unit that was destined to become the standard bearer during the decade, and again it was on Bernstein's Funny Car. Co-designed by Armstrong and Jim Faust, a prototype of the now immensely popular RacePak unit was on Bernstein's car as early as 1982.

The first unit was not terribly successful, but after consulting with Unlimited Hydroplane boat racer Ron Armstrong, co-owner of Race-Pak, things quickly changed. A new, refined version of the RacePak was in Bernstein's car for the beginning of the 1984 season, and it revolutionized drag-racing data recording. The RacePak monitored and stored 32 functions, including engine rpm, rear-axle speed, tyre spin, clutch slippage, supercharger pressure, manifold pressure and cylinder pressure.

By 1985, the RacePak was available to every racer for about $2,500, and the resultant data changed the face of drag racing. It led to more efficient clutch and fuel systems, spawned high-gear-only total-clutch-management drivetrains, and aerodynamic fine tuning.

▼ **When on-board data recorders were introduced to the sport in the mid-1980s, the complexion of drag racing was forever changed.**

Gone was the guesswork of the past. Crew chiefs and drivers were able to get an instant replay of their last lap – errors and all.

BLOW IT!

★ ★ ★

The 1980s began with the 10.71:1 supercharger as the blower of choice. Although crude – its original use was on trucks – it had been refined throughout the years and was still the best way of moving vast amounts of air into the engine without any throttle lag (such as is experienced with turbocharging). With the "more is better" theory running rampant through all the other areas of fuel racing, it was only natural that the same logic would be applied to superchargers.

Meyer surprised everyone at the 1981 Orange County International Raceway Manufacturers Meet when he showed up with a 12.71:1 supercharger on his Funny Car. Today's 14.71:1 units were originally planned for use in alcohol racing, but the fuel racers saw the benefits of using the bigger superchargers and quickly adopted them. Again, fearing that things would get out of hand, as they inevitably would have, the NHRA put a 14.71:1 limit on supercharger sizes in 1983.

The 14.71:1 Roots-type supercharger, however, does have its drawbacks. The Roots pressurizes the plenum by backflow, resulting in large amounts of heat in the air while at the same time draining horsepower from the crankshaft.

The supercharger is little more than a pressure cooker, and when bolted on top of a nitro-burning engine is prone to failure, usually in the form of a fiery explosion towards the finish line.

Knowing that supercharger explosions generally begin in the intake manifold, the NHRA introduced a rule for the beginning of the 1988 season that required a burst panel on all nitro-intake manifolds. Deve-

▲ Another item Dale Armstrong tried on Kenny Bernstein's Funny Car – never before seen – was a supercharger overdrive unit, effectively giving the supercharger another gear. The NHRA banned the unit before it even ran on the car.

loped by fuel-systems expert Waterman, the 10-square-inch (64.5-sq-cm) panel has a limit of 195 psi (about 1.3×10^6 pascals). When pressure within the manifold reaches that level, signalling an explosion, the panel ruptures, thereby allowing the rapidly expanding gases to escape before structure separation results.

◄ By the early 1980s supercharger technology had progressed to a stage where specialist companies were manufacturing hundreds of superchargers per day to supply the drag-racing market, including Mooneyham, Kuhl and Littlefield. The supercharger had also grown, current size/ratio being 14.71:1 as laid down by NHRA rules.

MINOR TEAM IN THE MINOR LEAGUE
★ ★ ★

Since teaming with agribusiness magnate Larry Minor at the beginning of the decade, Gary Beck had been a Winston Top Fuel Champion waiting to happen. He had been denied the title by small margins in 1980 and in 1981. Beck had also established himself as something of a barrier breaker by being the first driver to enter the 5.80-, 5.70- and 5.60-second zones, and at the close of the 1981 season, the 5.50-second zone. No one could dispute that the blue dragster, ably tuned by crew chief Bernie Fedderly, was capable of great things and spent much of its time on the track pushing the performance envelope.

In chasing the 1982 Winston Top Fuel title, Beck reset the National E.T. Record, recording a 5.54 at the 1982 U.S. Nationals. He also became the first driver to cover the standing-start quarter-mile in less than five-and-a-half seconds when he recorded a 5.48 quarter-mile later at the same race.

Despite his outstanding performance, Beck was denied the Winston title again. Shirley Muldowney, who won the 1982 U.S. Nationals title, used that victory as a springboard to her third career Championship.

However, in 1983, Beck, Minor and Fedderly were unstoppable. Minor, an experienced off-road racer, had a second car built for himself and the two cars became the terrors of the quarter-mile, qualifying at every race they attended. They even met in the final round of the 1983 Cajun Nationals, a race Minor won "by mistake".

Beck's car reset National Records again and again, and with it he scored his first event victory since the 1981 Winston Finals when he defeated Connie Kalitta for the 1983 Gatornationals title. Beck also

▲ **Through 1982 and 1983 Gary Beck was all but unbeatable. The transplanted Canadian won numerous National event titles — here he is pictured after capturing the 1983 Golden Gate Nationals title — and set performance records by the score.**

▼ **Larry Minor racing won its second Winston Top Fuel Championship in 1987 when Dick LaHaie fought a spirited season-long campaign with Joe Amato for the title.**

won the prestigious U.S. Nationals for a third time, and in doing so became the first low qualifier to win in Indy in 22 years.

On the way to claiming the Winston title, Beck set Low Elapsed Time of the Meet at 10 of the 12 National events held. He also ended the season with the distinction of having run the sport's 17 quickest elapsed times, including another barrier breaker, a first-into-the-5.30-second zone 5.391 at the 1983 Golden Gate Nationals. (The 17th-quickest run was a 5.511.) Minor was 18th quickest with a 5.513, and Beck had the 19th to 21st places. Beck's total domination earned him the Winston title by a 2,124-point margin. Former Alcohol Dragster racer Joe Amato, who had made the move to Top Fuel in 1982, finished second in the Championship chase.

Amato, a self-made millionaire of Italian descent, had been working with former Super Stock racer and engine builder Tim Richards, someone not many people had heard of. "Tim is the kind of guy that doesn't just take someone else's ideas and use them," Amato enthused; "He comes up with his own plan."

And Richards' plans were original, to say the least. During the following few years and into the 1990s, the one crew chief watched by every Top Fuel racer is Richards.

▼ **Gary Beck arrived at Minor's team with some impressive credentials, the Canadian having won the 1974 World title (the** forerunner of the Winston title), fending off Don Garlits for the honour.

LARRY THE BIG RACER

★ ★ ★

Since 1980, Minor has emerged as drag racing's most prolific car owner. Not only did he own the Top Fuel dragster driven by Beck, he owns the Funny Car driven by his longtime friend Ed McCulloch.

Minor, an experienced desert off-road-racing veteran, had a dragster built for himself in 1983 and won that year's Cajun Nationals, defeating none other than Beck in the final. Beck returned the compliment a year later.

However, fielding a two-car team can lead to complications, and a first-round victory over Beck at the 1984 U.S. Nationals almost certainly cost Beck that year's Winston Top Fuel title. Of course it helped Minor's standing in the season-long points chase, in which he came sixth.

After Minor parted company with Beck, his next driver, Dick LaHaie, drove his way to the 1987 Winston title, surviving a neck-and-neck battle with Joe Amato to take the Championship at the last race of the

▲ The ever-smiling Larry Minor. Besides being one of drag racing's most prolific car owners, Minor has taken a ride or two himself and actually won a couple of National events, the 1983 Cajun Nationals (beating Gary Beck, no less), and the 1986 Mile-High Nationals.

season. When LaHaie's three-year contract with the team was not renewed, Minor signed Muldowney as the team's Top Fuel representative in 1990. But Muldowney was never a factor in the Championship battle, and after one year she, too, was dropped from the team.

Perhaps Minor's biggest disappointment has come with his Funny Car team. Headed by veteran crew chief Fedderly, the McCulloch-driven entry is a threat wherever it races and has carried the team into the winner's circle at 12 NHRA National events. But as a result of parts breakage – usually of only minor components – the car has frequently been denied the Winston Funny Car title. In 1990, the team missed the title by just 456 points.

CRUZ MISSILE

★ ★ ★

Minor's latest Top Fuel jockey is Cruz Pedregon, a young driver of undoubted talent who is following in the footsteps of his father, the late "Flaming Frank" Pedregon.

Pedregon began drag racing trucks when he was 16 years old and, with help of the late Joe Pisano, had his first ride in an Alcohol Dragster by the time he was in his early 20s. But it was not until he teamed with car owner Gary Turner in 1989 that Pedregon really came to the fore. That year, he drove the Alcohol Dragster to two National event victories.

Feeling the need to broaden his horizons, Pedregon next drove the Miner Brothers Alcohol Funny Car. Again, he proved himself a natural driver, winning in his debut in the car at the 1990 Winternationals.

After one year in the Alcohol Funny Car, Pedregon had the urge to go fuel racing, and Larry Minor just happened to be looking for a driver. The two got acquainted, and as the well-worn saying goes, the rest is history.

Driving the car that Muldowney had used the year before, Pedregon earned his Top Fuel licence with a 5.03-second lap, the quickest ever run by a new driver. But despite running 4.99 at Houston Raceway Park in testing, the car was never a winner and was dropped in mid-1991 to make way for a new Al Swindahl car. The car was a surefire winner from the moment it was unloaded, and carried Pedregon to the semi-finals at the 1991 Northwest Nationals.

▼ **Larry Minor's latest driver is Cruz Pedregon. Pedregon perhaps offers Minor the most potential to repeat the heady days of the early 1980s, being one of the fastest-reacting drivers in the hot-rod world.**

▶ **For one brief year, 1990, Shirley Muldowney ran for the Larry Minor/Otter Pops Racing stable, although with little on-track success. Cruz Pedregon replaced Muldowney at the end of the 1990 season.**

▲ and ▶ The Ace in the pack. Longtime friend Ed McCulloch drives Larry Minor's Otter Pops-backed Funny Car. McCulloch, who has won numerous National event titles, has been thwarted in his attempts to win the Winston Funny Car Championship throughout his long and varied career.

PLAYING THE ACE
★ ★ ★

Known as "the Ace" McCulloch has been involved in drag racing since the early 1960s, driving everything from slingshot Top Fuel dragsters to his current Funny Car. One of the original Funny Car racers when the class was introduced in 1968, McCulloch had appeared in 38 final rounds at the close of the 1990 season, winning on 18 occasions. His first victory came at the 1971 U.S. Nationals, and his most recent was at the 1990 Winston Finals.

McCulloch teamed with Minor in 1984 after spending several seasons on the fringe of the sport driving uncompetitive cars. Since joining up with Minor, McCulloch has again become one of the most respected drivers in the class. He recorded the category's all-time quickest run of 5.132 seconds at the 1989 Chief Nationals.

If McCulloch had to pick a favourite racetrack, it would be Indianapolis Raceway Park, where he won the U.S. Nationals title five times, an event record in any category. After his initial victory in 1971, McCulloch went on to repeat the achievement in 1972, 1983, 1988 and 1990, all in the Funny Car category.

▼ **The one constant on Larry Minor's team throughout the 1980s and into the 1990s has been crew chief Bernie Fedderly, left, seen here with Ed McCulloch. As crew chief on McCulloch's Funny Car, Fedderly has become one of drag racing's most respected nitro-engine tuners.**

◄ This experiment was a winner right from the word go. Using a huge swept-back rear wing, which created a downward force on the car, Joe Amato cracked the magic 260 mph (418.42 km/h) barrier in March 1984.

▼ Never afraid to try something different, Joe Amato raced this unusual-looking Pontiac Alcohol Funny Car during the early years of the eighties. His willingness to experiment has made him one of the sport's leading exponents.

Joe Amato was not joking when he commented that his crew chief, Tim Richards, liked to come with his own ideas. One of Richards' ideas was to consider the use of aerodynamics in drag racing – or more to the point, the current lack of use of aerodynamics.

CHEATING THE WIND

★ ★ ★

At the 1984 Gatornationals, Richards introduced an aerodynamic trick on Amato's dragster that could not be hidden. It stood out like a Mini Metro in a fleet of Ferrari F40s. It was the wing – the rear wing, to be precise. Even if they had not gone to win the 1984 Winston Top Fuel Championship, Amato and Richards would be remembered for changing the face of Top Fuel drag racing.

◀ and ▼ The rear wing on Amato's Keystone/Hurst Shifter dragster boasted a huge 7½-feet (2.29-m) tall stabilizer wing mounted high above and behind the engine.

The rear wing on Amato's Keystone/Hurst Shifter dragster boasted a huge 7½-feet (2.29-m) tall stabilizer wing mounted high above and behind the engine. The thinking behind it was so simple that the only surprise was that it had never been tried before. Situated where it was, the wing was out of the way of the turbulence created by the motor and the rear tyres, and it would act by putting downward pressure on the rear tyres. At the time, cars like Gary Beck's would burn around 400 horsepower to achieve this effect. For Amato, the wing created a situation in which the motor wasted only 100 horsepower to get the required down pressure. The saved power translated into immediate speed gains.

At that race Amato became the first person in drag-racing history to crack the 260-mph (418.42-km/h) barrier using a piston-driven engine. He ran a 5.58 at 260.11 mph (418.60 km/h) to beat Gary Ormsby in the semifinals, then ran a 5.54 at 262.39 mph (422.26 km/h) to beat Beck in the final round.

At the next race on the tour, the Southern Nationals in April, every Top Fuel racer in the pits had a crude replica of Amato's Eldon Rasmussen-designed wing. But it mattered little. Amato and Richards had caught the other racers off guard, and it was not until early spring that the field began to catch up with them.

The use of aerodynamics had been tried before. From drag racing's formative years, racers had been trying to cheat the air. None, however, had stood the world on its collective head, like Richards and Amato, and most were abandoned after a couple of appearances.

▶ and ▼ The wing, dreamed up by crew chief Tim Richards, acted by putting downward pressure on the rear tyres — a task that hitherto wasted 400 hp of engine power.

TEMPO'S TIME HAD COME
★ ★ ★

Aerodynamic improvements were not restricted to the Top Fuel category. Once again, Kenny Bernstein and his crew chief, Dale Armstrong, were looking for more efficient ways to get their Ford Tempo-bodied Funny Car to cut through the air. Because of Bernstein's close ties with Ford, he became one of the first drag racers allowed to use the once inaccessible car-manufacturer's wind tunnels. After spending two days locked in the Lockheed wind tunnel, the car that emerged was one of the most advanced quarter-mile vehicles ever seen – regardless of category – and was head and shoulders more efficient than anything that had gone down a dragstrip.

The Tempo had rounded fenderwells, a lipped nose spoiler and side skirt, a belly pan, and full side windows to prevent air from getting inside and under the body. A tall rear spoiler – or whale deck as it became known – provided increased down-force without substantial drag. Bernstein's previous car, a Mercury LN-7, created 1,360 pounds (616.90 kg) of drag at 200 mph (321.86 km/h) but the Tempo created just 940 pounds (426.38 kg) at the same speed. That was an improvement of 45 per cent; the body alone was a full 10 per cent more efficient than the stock Tempo Funny Car body.

Needless to say, Bernstein, armed with this knowledge, became unbeatable in 1984, registering a third-place finish in the Winston Funny Car Championship chase before winning the first of four consecutive titles the following year.

BUICK DEBUT
★ ★ ★

Bernstein and Armstrong were not finished with aerodynamics, however. In 1987, they introduced a Buick LeSabre that looked nothing like a Funny Car (or an '87 LeSabre for that matter) ever did. It had a huge rear spoiler, a narrow roof, and a laid-back windscreen. It resembled a Porsche 962 more than a Buick. The car was legal, much to the NHRA's disappointment; it represented a rather liberal interpretation of the rules by adhering to the letter of the rulebook if not the spirit.

Perhaps the ultimate in aerodynamic efficiency, the car helped Bernstein rack up a 43-3 win-loss record from October 1986 to September 1987. In that time, he won 10 out of 12 events, and it was unquestionably Bernstein's most productive period.

Other racers duplicated Bernstein's ghastly LeSabre body, including Jim Head, John Force and Ed McCulloch. But none achieved the same success that Bernstein enjoyed. Obviously, Bernstein did not win all those races on aerodynamic trickery alone; plenty of horsepower helped to push the car through the air.

To ensure that Funny Car bodies would at least bear some resemblance to the showroom models they were based on, the NHRA clarified the 1988 body rules, and the Batmobile era was over.

At the same time as the aerodynamic trickery in the Funny Car ranks, the Top Fuel racers began looking again at what tricks would be attached to their cars to help them cheat the wind, thus spawning perhaps the sport's most creative period – the rebirth of the streamliners.

◄ **(and inset) When it made its first appearance in 1987 it quickly became known as the Batmobile. Kenny Bernstein's Buick LeSabre Funny Car was the ultimate in aerodynamic efficiency – and was something of a liberal interpretation of the NHRA rule book. The car was banned in 1988.**

► **When Kenny Bernstein's "Batmobile" first appeared, it did not take the other Funny Car racers too long to come out with their own versions. John Force's Castrol GTX Funny Car was perhaps the least wild of the interpretations.**

FUELLING THE RECOVERY

★ ★ ★

Ironically, this creative period came at a time when Top Fuel racing was at its lowest ebb. The class had been decimated in 1984.

Throughout that year the numbers of entries were down and at three races, the Springnationals, Summernationals and NorthStar Nationals, the fields fell short of the usual 16 cars. The Springnationals was further marred by a top-end spill involving racer Doug Kerhulas, who was seriously injured. Two weeks later, Shirley Muldowney had a near-fatal crash at Le Grandnational when her car jumped the guardrail just past the finishing line.

Adding to the category's woes, Amato and then number-three man in the standings, Jody Smart, ordered Funny Cars, seemingly ready to join the Candies & Hughes team, which had made the change in 1983. Number-five finisher Richard Tharp went sprint car racing. The IHRA dropped the class altogether in time for the beginning of the 1984 season, stating that there was not any interest in the category.

The category's spectacular recovery from its deathbed can be attri-

COEFFICIENT OF DRAG (Cd)

The lower the Cd number, the better an object cuts through the air — or at least, that is the theory. The lowest Cd numbers come from shapes that have the maximum body volume forward, tapering back towards the narrowest angle at the rear — in other words, a teardrop.

PARACHUTE	1.35 Cd
FLAT PLATE	1.17
CUBE	1.05
SEATED PERSON	0.60
MOTORCYCLE	0.57–0.80
CONVERTIBLE CAR	0.50–0.70
RAILWAY CARRIAGE	0.50
CITY BUS	0.45–0.50
SPORTS CAR	0.32–0.36
BIRD	0.30
BULLET	0.25–0.3
LAND SPEED RECORD CAR	0.11
TEAR DROP (3:1 length-to-thickness ratio)	0.04–0.05

▲ **Jim Head's outrageous Oldsmobile Firenza was the wildest of all the Funny Car creations, although neither his, or John Force's, could match the out-and-out performance of Kenny Bernstein's machine.**

◄ **Although many Top Fuel racers copied Joe Amato's tall rear wing, when the Key Auto Parts team introduced their car at the 1984 Gatornationals they had effectively given themselves a six-week advantage over the competition.**

buted to two incidents, unrelated except that they both occurred at the 1984 U.S. Nationals.

After sporadic visits to the NHRA tour since his "retirement" from drag racing in 1975, Don Garlits was back, with a vengeance. His last appearance had been at the 1984 Gatornationals, and he had not been heard of since. But with the help of Bradenton, Florida, track owner Art Malone, the two veterans of the sport had gathered what spares they had left and announced that they would race in Indy and at the remaining races on the tour. Better yet, they were already building a new race car for the 1985 season. As in all fairy tales a happy ending was in the script. Garlits won on his return, defeating his long-time rival, Connie Kalitta, in the final round.

The other incident was the announcement by Joe Hrudka, founder and president of Mr. Gasket, that two of his other companies, Cragar and Weld, would sponsor an exclusive Top Fuel Classic series in 1985.

Garlits and Malone remained true to their word. Besides racing at all the events in 1985, they had a sponsor, Super Shops, and pushed aside the opposition. Ever the crowd favourite, the king of the dragsters won six NHRA National events in 1985 and was crowned Winston Top Fuel Champion exactly 10 years after his first title. He then repeated the achievement in 1986, joining Muldowney as the only other three-time Winston Top Fuel Champion, and he won the U.S. Nationals title that year for an unprecedented third straight time. From his comeback in September 1984 to the end of the 1986 season, Garlits won 13 of 29 National events he entered. Top Fuel and Don Garlits were again very much alive and well.

DON GARLITS – 1986 WINSTON TOP FUEL CHAMPION

By winning the 1986 Winston Top Fuel title, beating Darrell Gwynn by 524 points, Don Garlits became only the second driver – Shirley

CHASSIS: Garlits
ENGINE: 8 cylinder aluminium JP-1
CAPACITY: 500 cu in (8.1 L)
COMPUTER-CALCULATED HORSEPOWER: 3,800 bhp @ 6,800 rpm
CYLINDER HEADS: 2-valve Dart
FUEL CONSUMED PER RUN: 1.49 gallons per second
TYRES: Goodyear
SPONSORS: Super Shops/ Garlits & Malone
BEST TIME: 5.34 seconds
BEST SPEED: 272.56 mph
EVENT VICTORIES:
Gatornationals 5.503 seconds 268.65 mph; NorthStar Nationals 5.562 seconds 259.36 mph; U.S. Nationals 5.399 seconds 266.66 mph; Chief Nationals 5.390 seconds 268.01 mph

Muldowney being the other – to win drag racing's most prestigious Championship three times.

Garlits had already set the tone for 1986 at the close of 1985 by announcing his intentions to take a crack at the 270-mph (434.51-km/h) barrier with a car the likes of which never had been seen before.

He was true to his word. At the 1986 Gatornationals – just 20 miles (32 km) from Garlits' home town of Ocala, Florida – he introduced Swamp Rat XXX, a semi-streamliner. Much as Garlits expected, the car cracked 270 mph with consummate ease,

running as fast as 272.56 (438.63 km/h) on the way to the event title. After a second victory of the year at the Cajun Nationals, Garlits suffered his first blowover at the Summernationals. He rebuilt the car and won back-to-back titles at the NorthStar Nationals and U.S. Nationals. His last victory of the year, at the Chief Nationals, put a grip on the Winston title.

Although he did not win the Winston Finals title, Garlits did win the Cragar/Weld Wheel Top Fuel Classic title, his final achievement before a second blowover in Spokane, Washington, put him into self-imposed retirement.

1

2

THE BLOWOVER

For all the sport's potential for disaster, accidents, especially in the Top Fuel category, are few and far between. It is a testament to the NHRA's strict safety requirements that when there is a spill, the driver more often than not walks away. If an accident does occur, the cause is usually traced back to the drive. Use of on-board data recorders often proves the point. Competitors, believing they can drive their way out of trouble, sometimes stay on the throttle a millisecond too long, and . . .

When the Top Fuellers breached the 270-mph barrier, a new phenomenon started to occur. Eventually dubbed "the blowover", drivers found that the front wheels of their race cars started to lift as they approached the finish line. For drivers travelling at more than 270 mph, this could present something of a problem.

The first to experience the blowover was Don Garlits, whose Swamp Rat XXX blew over backwards at Old Bridge Township Raceway Park, New Jersey, in 1986. Many so-called experts attributed the accident to Garlits' use of a spoon-shaped nose on the front of his dragster. However, in late 1987, when Richard Holcomb went over backwards in his more conventional-looking dragster questions were raised as to whether any car might go over. Garlits, by this time, had quit the sport. Another blowover, this time at a track in Spokane, Washington, had prompted the King of the Dragsters' early retirement.

At the start of the 1989 season Eddie Hill rode out perhaps the fastest blowover, his Super Shops/Pennzoil dragster hauling its rear wing across the finish line at 250 mph before somersaulting in mid-air. Hill's prang was attributed to the front wings vibrating loose at the mid-track point and falling into a negative angle of attack — in effect, encouraging the car to lift off the ground. Other racers have since joined the infamous 360-degree club, including Don Prudhomme, the late Gary Ormsby and Russ Collins, whose BME-backed dragster performed some mid-air ballet before slamming to earth in a tangle of twisted tubing. In all cases, the drivers climbed out from what was left of their respective race cars, shaken, sometimes bruised, but very much alive.

In 1986 drag-racing fans got their first look at a new phenomenon: the blowover. First in many things, Don Garlits rode out this blowover at the 1986 NHRA Summernationals at Old Bridge Township Raceway Park, New Jersey. Paired against Darrell Gwynn in a qualifying heat, Garlits' revolutionary Swamp Rat XXX has carried the front wheels away from the starting line before snapping skywards at mid-track (1). Past the point of no return, Garlits' car starts to pivot on its rear wing (2), before turning through 180 degrees and slamming back down to earth (3). Garlits is fortunate that the car lands the correct way up. He is able to regain control of the car and bring it to a safe halt (4). Garlits was uninjured and returned to racing two weeks later.

3

4

For a year or more, racers were content to copy and refine Joe Amato's big wing idea. It worked – well – and it was not expensive. But seeing what Kenny Bernstein and Dale Armstrong were up to set many racers thinking.

Streamliners had been tried in the past, but with little success. Racers back in the 1960s and 1970s adapted their ideas from the Bonneville Salt Flat lakesters and streamliners. Those ideas were suited to cars travelling over four or five miles (5–8 km) of racecourse, but they offered few advantages for cars travelling the straight-line quarter-mile.

The racers of the mid-1980s knew that having a slippery looking race car was not enough to achieve quicker elapsed times. The slippery shape had to be effective, and several racers began looking at the Indy car set and how ground-effects might be applied to drag racing.

▲ and ▶ Streamliners had been tried in the past – with varying degrees of success, or lack of it – but when Gary Ormsby's Castrol GTX streamliner appeared in 1986 it heralded a new chapter in drag racing history.

CASTROL GTX STREAMLINER
★ ★ ★

The first racer to sink a significant amount of money into a workable streamliner was Gary Ormsby who, with help from sponsor Castrol GTX, introduced his aerodynamically advanced race car at the 1986 Winternationals.

The body was built from carbon fibre and featured an Indy Car-style cockpit. Along with the unusual nose and wing designs, this gave the car an unmistakable March-car look. The final design was the result of dimensions fed into an aircraft design computer, which provided a three-dimensional drawing and simulated wind-tunnel testing. Eloisa Garza, part of the Jim Hall/Johnny Rutherford Indy Car team that won the 1981 Indy 500, created the body, which was mounted on an Al Swindahl chassis. Without a doubt, it was an amazing vehicle that looked as though it was doing 270 mph (434.51 km/h) standing still, which was the target for the car.

As new rides usually do, the Castrol streamliner suffered from new-car troubles. At its debut at the 1986 Winternationals, the car's super-charger exploded on the burnout. The team later learned that the magnetos were earthing out on the carbon fibre bodywork, which triggered the explosion.

Then came Garlits.

CASTROL GTX STREAMLINER TECH SHEET	
CAR	Castrol GTX Special
CHASSIS	Swindahl
ENGINE	489-cubic-inch (8-litre) Keith Black
CRANKSHAFT	Crower
SUPERCHARGER	Mooneyham
INTAKE MANIFOLD	Cragar
CYLINDER HEADS	Dart
IGNITION	Mallory
SPARK PLUGS	NGK
HEADERS	Hedman
TRANSMISSION	Lenco
CLUTCH	Crower

▼ Conceived with the aid of an aircraft computer, and featuring futuristic nose and wing designs, the Castrol GTX streamliner had the feel of an old-style Indy car.

► It was not too often that a racer would go the whole hog and build a complete stream-liner, as Abrams and Schacker did in 1986. However, like racers before them, they found their Alcohol Dragster a little too unpredictable and retired the car before any realistic performances were turned in.

GARLITS AND THE SWAMP RAT XXX

★ ★ ★

Garlits was a man with a mission in the early part of the 1986 season. He wanted to be the first racer to break the 270-mph (434.51-km/h) barrier, and he wanted to do it badly. He had already achieved 268.01 mph (431.31 km/h) at the 1985 Winston Finals, and he had hoped to run 270 mph at the 1986 Winternationals. But his promised new car – which he claimed would turn everyone's heads – was not quite ready.

When he introduced Swamp Rat XXX at the Gatornationals a few weeks later, no one was ready for what they saw. The most notable feature on the self-built car was the nose, which was shaped like a teaspoon and housed the 14-gallon (53-litre) fuel tank. Rather than having the usual motorcycle-type front wheels, Garlits' car had spun aluminium discs that were wrapped by rubber belts (he could not get tyres small enough). The other item that caught the eye was the fully enclosed cockpit, which Garlits claimed was an aerodynamic and safety feature rolled into one. Garlits expected the Lexan shield to become standard equipment on all dragsters within six months of development, and he was proved right.

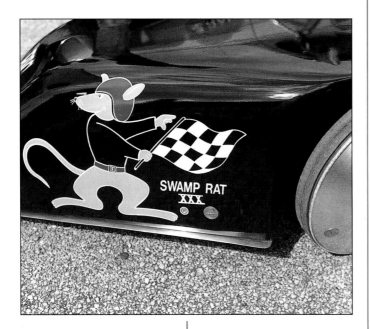

◄ **Another racer to try the canopy was Connie Kalitta. The canopy was a temporary fad, however, and by the turn of the decade few racers were using one.**

▲ ►**Not a true streamliner – it was dubbed a semi-liner by most observers – Don Garlits' Swamp Rat XXX was by far the most successful of all the attempts at cheating the wind. Distinguished by its spoon-like front nose and little front wheels, it enabled Garlits to break the 270-mph (434.51-km/h) barrier in March 1987 on the car's National event debut.**

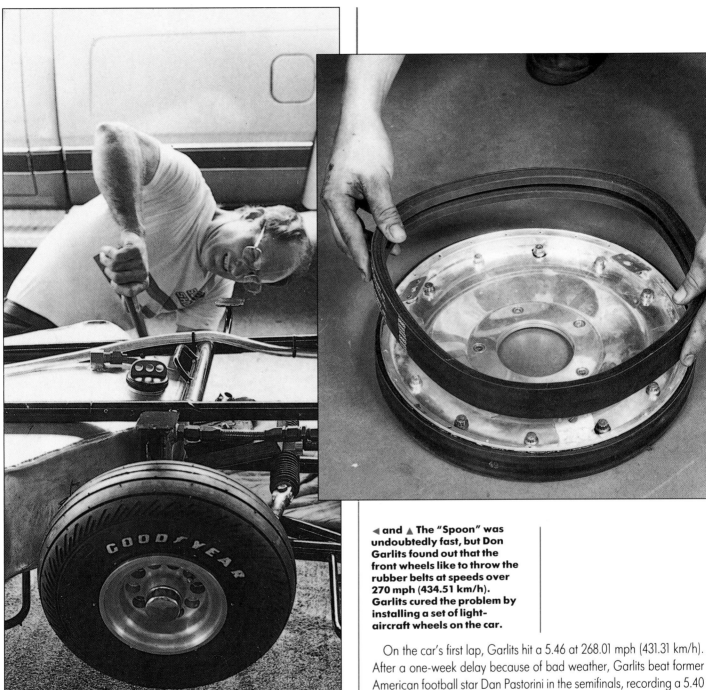

◄ and ▲ The "Spoon" was undoubtedly fast, but Don Garlits found out that the front wheels like to throw the rubber belts at speeds over 270 mph (434.51 km/h). Garlits cured the problem by installing a set of light-aircraft wheels on the car.

Although many people scoffed when they first saw Garlits' car, "Big Daddy" knew exactly what he was doing. His car was unquestionably a streamliner, but he had not gone the whole way and included engine canopies and rear-wheel flares. Knowing that weight would be a factor, his latest car weighed exactly the same as his previous car.

On the car's first lap, Garlits hit a 5.46 at 268.01 mph (431.31 km/h). After a one-week delay because of bad weather, Garlits beat former American football star Dan Pastorini in the semifinals, recording a 5.40 at 272.56 mph (438.63 km/h). Garlits had achieved what he had set out to do, and the streamliner's future was assured. Or so it seemed.

Garlits' car was a success, especially after he replaced the rubber belts with light aircraft wheels and tyres under the nose of the car. Despite a blowover at the Summernationals in July, Garlits came back and won five events on the way to the 1986 Winston Top Fuel title.

Ormsby's car was not so successful, and was retired after the 1987 Southern Nationals. The two cars competed twice, and both times Garlits' semi-liner, as it was becoming known, won. Their last duel was

► After experimenting with the spoon-shaped front nose the next thing Joe Amato tried was the canopy – as did several other racers. However, like the spoon, Amato rejected this idea and returned to running a conventional dragster.

◄ Streamlining 1991 style. At the start of the 1991 season Joe Amato experimented with this Mike Magiera-designed package which worked from the start. Without the rear wing, Amato recorded a 5.05 at Houston Raceway Park, but the package was never tried again as Amato concentrated on the Winston Championship chase.

▶ and ▼ ▶ The Mike Magiera-designed ground-effects package was also tried on Kenny Bernstein's Top Fuel dragster during 1991. Like his rival Joe Amato, however, Bernstein tried the package on only rare occasions as he too became embroiled in a heated Winston championship title points battle.

at the 1986 Cajun Nationals, where the two met in the first — and so far only — all-streamliner final round.

Garlits' success prompted several drivers to try the streamliner route. The most notable racer to hop onto the bandwagon was Joe Amato, who introduced a car strikingly similar to Garlits', ran it once (at the 1986 NorthStar Nationals), did not like its handling characteristics at the top end, and promptly parked it forever.

Darrell Gwynn, a former Alcohol Dragster racer who had moved up to Top Fuel in 1985 and then joined forces with the Budweiser team of Kenny Bernstein, introduced a monstrous-looking streamliner at the

1987 Winternationals. The car was unbelievably heavy, and race by race more of the streamlining body panels were taken off until it looked more like a conventional dragster. Without the extra weight, the car was a flyer and chalked up unprecedented elapsed times, culminating in a 5.28 at the 1986 Chief Nationals.

The writing was on the wall. Streamliners looked good, but the extra weight added to the car could not be overcome by aerodynamic trickery. In drag racing, it was still better to bully the car down the track. Even Garlits, streamlining's strongest proponent, agreed. "It doesn't seem to be a good idea in drag racing anymore, does it?" he said.

Despite the advances being made in aerodynamics, not to mention engine tuning, a sub-five-second time was still considered impossible as late as 1987.

Darrell Gwynn's 5.28 at the 1986 Chief Nationals was unquestionably amazing, but most people thought that the Top Fuel dragster had reached its peak.

THE CREW CHIEF'S SECRET

★ ★ ★

As it had been for years, the secret was in the fuel system and the clutch. If a crew chief could organize those two pieces of hardware so that one would complement the other effectively, the world was his or hers. And as he had through most of the 1980s, Dale Armstrong was leading the field once again.

Besides tuning Kenny Bernstein's Funny Car, Armstrong was providing a tune-up for Gwynn, who had joined Bernstein's Budweiser team in 1986. With Armstrong's undoubted expertise, Gwynn led the assault on the record books. At the 1987 Gatornationals, Gwynn clocked 5.22 in qualifying. A month later at the Southern Nationals, he ran even quicker, recording a 5.204-second lap. A couple of weeks later, he dipped into the teens, running a 5.176 at the Texas Motorplex during the Winston All-Stars event.

How much quicker could a Top Fuel dragster go? Dick LaHaie, who was on his way to a first – and so far only – Winston Top Fuel Championship, responded with a 5.171 at the Summernationals. Then Joe Amato, the 1984 Winston Top Fuel Champion, joined the race. Amato had already assured himself a place in the record books in early September when he recorded the sport's first 280-mph lap at the U.S. Nationals, where he reached 282.13 mph (454.03 km/h) during eliminations. With crew chief Tim Richards calling all the shots, Amato joined the race for the four-second zone at the next event on the tour, the

▲ **With help from former opponent Shirley Muldowney, Don Garlits took a crack at the 4-second zone in October 1989. He fell just short, recording a career-best 5.07 on his one and only run in the car.**

▼ **By the end of the 1991 season, Joe Amato had run more 4-second laps than the rest of the 4-second runners combined. Much of that mechanical credit goes to his crew chief, Tim Richards, left.**

Keystone Nationals. There, he recorded a 5.171 during testing, then achieved a 5.118 the next day during qualifying – the first sub-teen five-second run in history.

Anticipation was high that at the next event on the calendar, the Chief Nationals at the Texas Motorplex, a track that has become synonymous with the best elapsed times since it opened in 1986, someone would do a five-zero-second run. Amato obliged by recording a 5.090 in qualifying.

It did not stop there. That number was surpassed when, during eliminations, Gwynn again took up the challenge and achieved an even quicker 5.084.

AN OUTSIDER BREAKS THROUGH

★ ★ ★

When the 1988 season opened, racers were openly talking about who would run the sport's first four-second elapsed time. Many assumed it would be Amato, Gywnn or, possibly, LaHaie. Most never even considered Eddie Hill.

Hill, one of the original drag racers in the mid-1950s, had been racing drag boats for most of the 1970s and early 1980s. It was on water that he established himself as something of a speed merchant, setting track and National Records everywhere he raced. He made the fastest pass ever by a propeller-driven boat at 229.00 mph (368.53 km/h), a record that still stood in 1991.

Drag-boat racing, however, is not without its dangers. A 217-mph (349.22-km/h) spill at Firebird Lake in Arizona prompted Hill to call it a day and return to the asphalt quarter-mile. He made his return at the 1985 Mile-High Nationals. Three years later, still an outsider, Hill unleashed a 5.066 at the 1988 Gatornationals and suddenly became the favourite and the name on everyone's lips.

One month later at the Texas Motorplex, which now was run by the IHRA courtesy of Billy Meyer, Hill broke perhaps one of the last true performance barriers. On 9 April he drove his Super Shops/Pennzoil-backed dragster to a 4.990. The four-second barrier had been broken.

Hill's achievement deflated many other drivers, including Amato and Gwynn, who believed that they should have broken the four-second mark. There were no sour grapes – far from it, everyone was happy for Hill – but it certainly knocked the wind out of other racers' sails.

▲ **The four-father. Eddie Hill beat both favourites Joe Amato and Darrell Gwynn to the 4-second zone. The former drag-boat racer recorded a history-making 4.99 on 9 April 1988.**

▼ **After being the first racer into the 4-second zone, Eddie Hill amazingly "lost" his combination and struggled through 1989 and 1990 before coming back with a vengeance during the 1991 season, running fours apparently at will.**

JOE AMATO – 1990 WINSTON TOP FUEL CHAMPION

The 1990 Winston Top Fuel title was decided in the last race of the last event of the year. In one lane was defending series Champion Gary Orsmby; Joe Amato was in

CHASSIS: Al Swindahl

ENGINE: 8 cylinder aluminium Keith Black

CAPACITY: 500 cu in (8.1 L)

COMPUTER-CALCULATED HORSEPOWER: 5,400 bhp @ 6,800 rpm

CYLINDER HEADS: 2-valve Dart

FUEL CONSUMED PER RUN: 2.02 gallons per second

TYRES: Goodyear

SPONSORS: Valvoline/Key Auto Parts

BEST TIME: 4.935 seconds

BEST SPEED: 291.26 mph

EVENT VICTORIES: Arizona Nationals 5.052 seconds 275.14 mph; Mile-High Nationals 5.102 seconds 275.48 mph; NorthStar Nationals 4.970 seconds 273.39 mph; U.S. Nationals 5.042 seconds 270.83 mph; Heartland Nationals 5.040 seconds 272.14 mph; Winston Finals 4.935 seconds 282.39 mph

the other. The racers were tied in the points chase. The winner of the quarter-mile dash would win the event and collect from Winston the $150,000 bonus cheque for the Series Champion.

The race was over before it began. Ormsby could not wait for the green light, and Amato sprinted to a 4.93 for his third Winston Top Fuel Championship. That victory put him in the lofty company of Shirley Muldowney and Don Garlits, the only other three-time winners of the Series.

Amato fought neck-and-neck with Ormsby throughout the 1990 season, in which both drivers scored six National event victories. Victories at the Arizona Nationals (formerly the Fallnationals), Mile-High Nationals, NorthStar Nationals, U.S. Nationals, Heartland Nationals and the Winston Finals were enough to earn Amato the title.

"THE SNOWMAN" STRIKES

★ ★ ★

Almost unbelievably, neither Amato nor Gwynn was the second driver into the 4-Second Club. Gene Snow, a former Funny Car racer of some renown in the early 1970s, beat them to it when he produced a 4.997 at the NHRA Supernationals at another Texas track, Houston Raceway Park. Still, it was Hill who again stole the headlines. In beating Amato in the final round of that race, Hill recorded a 4.936, a run that even as the sport moves through the 1990s remains one of the quickest of all time.

Apart from the advances made in clutch and fuel-system technology, the car's length had increased from a standard 270 inches (685.8 cm) in 1987 to 300 inches (762.00 cm) in 1988, and this helped the dragsters to break the four-second barrier. Not all racers were convinced that longer was better. Hill's car, for instance, was only 288 inches (731.52 cm) long. But for the most part, new competitive dragsters had a 300-inch chassis (the maximum allowed by the NHRA), which allowed for better engine placement.

◄ **With a driving career that spans four decades, Shirley Muldowney is one of the sport's more charismatic figures, having won three Winston Top Fuel titles and numerous event titles, and has even had a movie made about her life story, "Heart Like A Wheel".**

▲ **With Eddie Hill's 4-second run being recorded at the Texas Motorplex — which was under IHRA management at the time — Gene Snow gave the NHRA their first 4-second run at Houston Raceway Park in October 1988.**

Although drag racing is not restricted in Top Fuel dragsters, the near-300-mph (480-km/h) landlocked missiles are indeed the sport's glamour category, much like Formula 1 cars and World of Outlaws sprint cars are the kings of the circuit races and the dirt tracks, respectively.

To cater for every driver's individual need for speed, however, the NHRA has created and nurtured 11 other categories, ranging from nitro-burning Funny Cars, capable of Top Fuel-like performance, to Pro Stock Motorcycles, the only two-wheel category recognized by the sanctioning body, to 11-second Super Street vehicles.

The categories are split into two distinct groups, Professional and Sportsman. The reasoning for the split is that the Pros – those who drive Top Fuel dragsters, Funny Cars, Pro Stockers and Pro Stock Motorcycles – race full-time for a living. The Sportsman competitors, those in Alcohol Dragster, Alcohol Funny Car, Competition Eliminator, Super Stock, Stock, Super Comp, Super Gas and Super Street, are weekend-only racers who cannot afford to make the financial commitment to racing in one of the Pro classes. This can be, however, something of a misnomer. Dozens of Sportsman racers spend a small fortune racing their cars, sometimes matching and even exceeding the amount a Professional racer would spend on his or her racing operation.

TOP FUEL

Unmistakable in appearance, the Top fuel dragster is everyone's lasting image of a dragster. It has big wheels at the rear and small wheels at the front. It is the ultimate hot rod. The 25-foot (7.62-m) vehicles are the fastest accelerating cars in the world, capable of covering the standing-start quarter-mile in 4.8 seconds at speeds in excess of 290 mph (466.70 km/h).

NHRA National Elapsed-time Record: 4.897 seconds – Joe Amato, Gainesville Raceway, Gainesville, Florida, March 1991.

NRHA National speed Record: 294.88 mph – Gary Ormsby, Texas Motorplex, Ennis, Texas, October 1989.

All National Records must be backed up within 1 per cent.

▼ **Before any race car is allowed on the track, it must first pass a rigorous technical inspection. Here, Jim White's Funny Car – the fastest of the breed with a 289.94 mph** **(466.60 km/h) lap recorded in mid-September 1991 – has his rear spoiler checked for correct height and width.**

FUNNY STORIES
★ ★ ★

When the 1980s opened, only four drivers had sat in a Funny Car and covered the quarter-mile in less than six seconds: Don Prudhomme, who ran a 5.98 at Ontario Motor Speedway in Ontario, California, in 1975; Raymond Beadle, also at 5.98 at the 1979 U.S. Nationals in Indianapolis, Indiana; Pat Foster; and Gordie Bonin. Today, more Alcohol Funny Car drivers have recorded five-second runs.

Not surprisingly, as Top Fuel performance times fell, so did those of Funny Cars. Two soon-to-be crew chiefs led the assault on the Record books at the beginning of the 1980s. Dale Armstrong (now Top Fuel driver Kenny Bernstein's crew chief) was the first into the 5.80s, and Tom Anderson (currently Funny Car driver Al Hofmann's crew chief) recorded the category's first 5.70-second lap.

Bernstein, unquestionably the Funny Car star of the 1980s, was first into the 5.60s (at 5.67), with no small amount of tuning help from Armstrong, who took over as crew chief in 1981. Rick Johnson surprised everyone when he cracked the 5.50 zone in one of Roland Leong's many entries over the years, getting a 5.58 at the 1985 Winternationals.

From there, Bernstein set the record-breaking pace. With the aid of an aerodynamically improved Ford Tempo, Bernstein managed to record the Funny Car category's first sub-5.50-second run, a 5.425 at the Texas Motorplex in 1986.

Then, with an even faster Buick LeSabre, Bernstein plunged into the 5.30s, running 5.397, 5.368 and 5.364 in the following year on 5 April, again at the Motorplex.

It was a surprise, therefore, that Bernstein was not the first Funny Car racer into the 5.20s. That honour went to Ed McCulloch, who drove the

FUNNY CAR
Although based on current Detroit models, Funny Cars bear little resemblance to their showroom counterparts. The only similarities are the tail-lights and badges. Using an identical engine to that of the Top Fuel dragster (mounted in front of the driver rather than behind), the 4,000-horsepower race cars are capable of running 5.1-second laps at speeds of just over 290 mph (466.70 km/h).
NHRA National Elapsed-time Record: 5.140 seconds — Jim White, Texas Motorplex, Ennis, Texas, October 1990.
NHRA National speed Record: 290.13 mph — Jim White, Texas Motorplex, Ennis, Texas, October 1991.
All National Records must be backed up within 1 per cent.

Larry Minor/Miller High Life Olds Cutlass to a 5.252 at Houston Raceway Park in Houston, Texas, in early October 1987. Predictably, Bernstein was not far behind. He recorded a 5.295 a couple of weeks later at Pomona Raceway in Pomona, California.

Conspicuously absent from the record books during this period of Funny Car development was one of the sport's more recognizable drivers: Don "the Snake" Prudhomme. Prudhomme had dominated the category during the mid- to late-1970s, winning an unprecedented four consecutive Funny Car titles. However, when sponsorship money began to dry up, Prudhomme became less and less competitive and sat out the 1986 season because of lack of sponsorship funds.

He returned to the sport the following year with backing from U.S. Tobacco's Skoal brand, and on 2 March 1989 recorded the category's first 5-teen, a 5.193 at Houston Raceway Park in Houston, Texas.

▶ **Long known as one of the fastest Funny Cars in the world, the JP-1 Special, campaigned by the late Joe Pisano, was unbeatable in its day. With Mike Dunn at the wheel, the car achieved the category's first recorded 280 mph (450.60 km/h) lap at the Texas Motorplex in October 1987.**

PRO (NOT SO) STOCK

★ ★ ★

Perhaps the most complex of drag racing's categories is Pro Stock, dubbed the factory hot rods by the sport's traditionalists. Pro Stock is one of the few categories in which Detroit's involvement is felt at a racing level. The big three American manufacturers – Ford, Dodge and General Motors – are involved in the category in some way.

At the beginning of the 1980s, the category was controlled by a complex series of weight limits, and racers were restricted to small-block power plants. In March 1980, the late Lee Shepherd recorded the quickest run ever for the petrol-burning race cars with an 8.37-second lap. At the end of the 1991 season, Warren Johnson held the National Record in one of his Oldsmobile Cutlasses at 7.180 seconds.

To be fair to Shepherd, Johnson was using a completely different engine combination with fewer restrictions than was Shepherd. In time for the beginning of the 1982 season, the NHRA made its rules like those of the IHRA – which at the time was running a successful Pro Stock Programme – and introduced a 500-cubic-inch (8.2-litre) two four-barrel carburettor rule that instantly trimmed the performance of the cars by more than a quarter of a second. Shepherd, who began the year by recording the category's quickest run, soon established himself as the class leader in the Reher-Morrison Chevrolet Camaro with a 7.86-second lap at the 1982 Winternationals.

From that race on, Shepherd and his arch rival Bob Glidden, driver of a series of Motorcraft Parts-backed Ford entries, dominated the category. Shepherd was the first into the 7.70s with a 7.78 at the 1982 Gatornationals. Seven months later, he broke the 7.60 barrier with a 7.69 at the Golden Gate Nationals. The 7.50s were not so easy to achieve. It took Shepherd more than two years to break into the zone, and his 7.59-second run recorded at the Citrus Nationals in West Palm Beach, Florida, in December 1984 was yet another record-breaking achievement to add to the list.

PRO STOCK

About the only things a modern-day Pro Stock car have in common with the showroom model it is based on are four wheels and a steering wheel. Hidden beneath the sleek fibreglass body panels are 500-cubic-inch (8.2-litre) race engines that breathe via two four-barrel carburettors. Radical chassis and suspension changes enable the cars to lap in the 7.1-second range at finishing-line speeds in excess of 190 mph (305.77 km/h).

NHRA National Elapsed-time Record: 7.180 seconds – Warren Johnson, Maple Grove Raceway, Pennsylvania, September 1991.

NHRA National Speed Record: 193.21 mph – Bob Glidden, Sears Points International Raceway, Sonoma, California, July 1991.

All National Records must be backed up within 1 per cent.

Three weeks before the 1985 Gatornationals, Shepherd was killed in a testing accident. Glidden, who had played second fiddle to his friendly rival for four years, established himself as the class leader. The first sub-7.5-second run was recorded at the 1985 Keystone Nationals as Glidden clocked a 7.497-second lap. Just less than a year later, at the 1986 U.S. Nationals, Glidden achieved a 7.377.

With the 7.4-second barrier broken, improvements were made in mere thousandths of a second as racers edged towards the 7.2-second zone. Unheralded Frank Sanchez stole everyone's thunder when he clocked a 7.294 at Houston Raceway Park in October 1988. Glidden lowered the record to 7.256, again at Houston Raceway Park, in March 1989. Mark Pawuk enjoyed his 15 minutes of fame (actually, it

▼ **Bob Glidden is the undisputed Pro Stock king. With 80 National event victories in his long career – most of them at the wheel of a Ford – he entered the 1990s** **as the driver with most wins ever in National event competition.**

lasted six months) when he recorded 7.220 at the 1990 Supernationals in his Oldsmobile Cutlass.

Then Darrell Alderman took over.

Alderman, driving the Mopar Parts/Wayne County Speed Shop Dodge Daytona, came to prominence at the end of the 1990 racing season with a string of dominating performances that ultimately carried him to the Winston Pro Stock title. In the first of these performances, he recorded a 7.206 at Heartland Park Topeka during the Heartland Nationals. One week later, while competing at the Texas Motorplex, he lowered the record even further, to 7.184, to astound everyone. John-

son's 7.180, at the 1991 Keystone Nationals, is the only quicker run.

Johnson, however, is the undisputed king of the finishing line, where the Georgia engine builder regularly clocks up Top Speed honours. Johnson was the first Pro Stock racer to go more than 180 mph (289.67 km/h) with a 181.08-mph (291.41-km/h) run at the 1982 Golden Gate Nationals. Glidden beat Johnson to the 190-mph (305.77-km/h) barrier with a 191.32-mph (307.89-km/h) run at the 1987 U.S. Nationals, and is still the National Record holder at 193.72 (311.75 km/h), recorded at the 1991 California Nationals. However, Johnson has recorded more runs in excess of 190 mph than most other Pro Stock racers combined.